Keeping Clean

Paul Bennett

Thomson Learning
New York

Nature's Secrets

Cover: A blue titmouse has a bath to keep its feathers clean.

Title page: A cleaner wrasse cleans a flame dwarf angel fish.

Contents page: A starling bathes in a puddle of water.

First published in the
United States in 1995 by
Thomson Learning
115 Fifth Avenue
New York, NY 10003

Published simultaneously in Great Britain by
Wayland (Publishers) Ltd.

U.K. copyright © 1995 Wayland (Publishers) Ltd.

U.S. copyright © 1995 Thomson Learning

Library of Congress Cataloging-in-Publication Data
Bennett, Paul, 1954–
  Keeping clean. / Paul Bennett.
     p.   cm.—(Nature's secrets)
  Includes bibliographical references (p.   ) and index.
  ISBN 1-56847-359-1
  1. Grooming behavior in animals—Juvenile litera-
ture. [1. Animals—Grooming behavior.] I. Title.
II. Series: Bennett, Paul, 1954–   Nature's secrets.
QL760.B45   1995
591.51—dc20   94-24312

Printed in Italy

Picture acknowledgments
The publishers would like to thank the following for allowing their photographs to be reproduced in this book: Bruce Coleman Ltd *cover*, 29 (main/Kim Taylor), *title page*, 11/both, 27 & 28/bottom (Jane Burton), 7 (top/Jeff Foott Productions), 7 (bottom/Bill Wood), 10 (A.J. Deane), 14 (Nigel Blake), 15 (top/John Shaw), 16, 24, (Leonard Lee Rue), 17 (top/Stephen C. Kaufman), 20 (Johnny Johnson), 21 (top/David Meredith), 22 (Erwin & Peggy Bauer), 23/top, 26, 29/inset (Dr Frieder Sauer); Heather Angel 18, 28/top; National History Photographic Agency 4 (Dr Ivan Polunin), 9 (bottom/Peter Johnson), 12 (Stephen Dalton), 13 (top/John Shaw), 13 (bottom/George Gainsborough), 17 (main/Rich Kirchner), 19 (Laurie Campbell), 21 (bottom/Nigel Dennis), 25 (top/Henry Ausloos), 25 (bottom/A.N.T. © K. Griffiths), 27 (top/Stephen Kraseman); Oxford Scientific Films *contents page* (Stan Osolinski), 5 (Tom McHugh), 6 (Sean Morris), 8 (John Netherton), 15 (bottom/Martyn Colbeck), 23 (main/Richard Packwood); Wayland Publishers Ltd 9 (top/Colin Milkins).

Contents

Care and attention

How many times a day do you wash your face and hands and clean your teeth? When do you have a bath or shower? Do you wash your hair once or more times a week? We keep ourselves clean to remove the dirt and germs that can cause illness and to keep our skin, hair, and teeth healthy.

Animals, too, must keep themselves clean. They do not use soap, shampoo, or toothpaste, but may lick, scratch, rub, nibble, pick, or bathe in water or shake themselves. Grooming – paying care and attention to the surface of the body – is important to the survival of an animal.

△ A flying gecko licks its eye with its tongue. Most geckos do not blink, so they use their tongues to remove dirt from their eyes.

◁ A macaque monkey cleans its injured arm. Animals will lick a wound to keep it clean and help it to heal properly. Scientists believe that saliva has healing properties.

△ A harvest mouse washes her newborn. Animals that are born helpless have to be cleaned by their mothers.

△ A sea otter lives entirely at sea and must keep its furry coat in good condition if it is to survive in its cold, watery world. This one is grooming by pressing its fur between its forepaws.

Most fish do not groom themselves, but some fish help other fish stay clean. This cleaner wrasse picks parasites off the skin, gills, fins, and even from inside the mouths of other fish. ▷

Preening

Feathers are very important to the well-being of birds. Without them, birds would not be able to fly. Feathers also provide protection from the rain and help to keep birds warm during the winter. Preening is a bird's way of taking care of its feathers.

◁ An elegant snowy egret preens itself. Feathers need to be kept in good condition and in the right position if they are to be useful for flying.

Feathers are very light and are made up of a central shaft and a flat part, or vane. The vane has thousands of tiny hooks and when it gets out of shape, the bird simply zips the vane back into shape by drawing the feather through its beak. ▷

Ducks and other waterbirds, such as this Adélie penguin, take oil from a preen gland near their tail. They spread the oil over the feathers to make them waterproof. ▽

Licking and nibbling

A mammal's furry coat gives good protection against the cold and rain. Fur also traps dirt and dead skin. To keep it in tip-top condition, the animal often takes some time to lick and nibble its fur.

◁ Cats are very supple and can reach most parts of their bodies easily. Their rough, sandpaper-like tongues help to remove any dirt and loose hairs and comb their fur into shape.

The brown rat uses its paws to ▷ reach those difficult places behind the ears and face. It licks its forepaws to moisten them and then brushes them over its head. Using its teeth, the brown rat nibbles its fur. The teeth work as tweezers to remove debris and dirt and also act as a kind of comb to untangle hairs. ▽

◁ An Indian fruit bat licks itself clean while hanging upside-down from its roost. The saliva, or spit, from the bat's mouth makes its fur slightly damp, but it soon dries out and becomes fluffy again.

The large-eared blacktail jack-rabbit pays careful attention to its paws. They need to be kept clean and healthy since the jackrabbit relies on them to run fast and escape from hungry enemies. ▷

A gecko sheds its old skin to reveal a shiny new one underneath. Lizards shed their skin from time to time in order to allow more room for growth. Some remove loose pieces of skin with their mouths and eat them. ▽

Scratching and rubbing

Many animals scratch their fur or skin with their hind legs when they groom. Animals also scratch or rub themselves to get rid of an itch and then return to whatever they were doing. Scratching and rubbing is also a good way of removing loose hair or skin.

△ A puffin balances on one foot as it scratches its face with its other foot.

14

An impala scratches the back of its head with its hind leg. Dust and biting flies irritate the skin of many African animals. ▷

Elephants are not very supple so they find it hard to scratch their huge bodies themselves. They often look for something large, such as a tree, to rub themselves on. This African elephant has found a termite mound on which to rub its stomach. ▽

◁ With its long arms and flexible body, the vervet monkey finds it easy to scratch itself. Its soft fur is probably home to fleas and other parasites.

Sometimes scratching is not enough to remove an itch. This Arctic ground squirrel is biting its tail to remove the cause of the irritation. ▽

A majestic caribou is rubbing off the velvet – the antler's furry covering – from its antlers. When the antlers have finished growing, the velvet dries up and is shed. ▷

The mighty brown bear takes time to scratch its head. It has long, sharp claws which are ideal for combing through its thick, brown fur. ▽

Bathing

Strangely enough, many animals not only bathe to get themselves clean, but they also bathe by deliberately getting themselves dirty. Both are ways of caring for the skin, fur, or feathers.

◁ A Japanese macaque grooms itself in a hot pool. This monkey lives on rocky hillsides and mountains, where the temperature can be very cold.

△ A sparrowhawk bathes in a puddle
of water to remove the dust and dirt
from its feathers.

◁ An African elephant blasts a cloud of dust from its trunk. In hot, dry weather, the elephant's skin is covered with insects and mites. Dust helps to clean its skin of these irritating pests.

A warthog wallows in mud. A good mud pack will protect its skin from heat and biting insects. ▽

△ A sparrow's dust bath acts as a dry shampoo. It shakes dust over its feathers, which helps to loosen dirt and parasites.

Mutual grooming

Mutual grooming is when one animal cleans another in its group. The helper can groom those difficult-to-reach places. It also encourages good relationships between the animals. The high-ranking or dominant individuals often demand to be groomed by lower-ranking ones.

◁ A black-face vervet concentrates as it looks for blood-sucking insects. Monkeys, apes, and lemurs use their nimble fingers and mouths to remove parasites from each other's fur. It keeps these mammals clean and everyone learns their place within the group.

An impala nibbles the neck of a friend. Mutual grooming is a good way of cleaning the neck and back. ▷

Zebras often find a tree to rub themselves on, but for those parts which are tricky to scratch, mutual grooming is very helpful. ▽

△ A mountain lion is
greeted with a bout of
licking. Being groomed
seems to be a relaxing and
pleasurable experience.

△ Spoonbills use their long beaks during bouts of mutual preening. The bond between male and female animals is made stronger during mutual grooming.

Rainbow lorikeets often live together in large flocks and preen each other as they sit on a branch. ▷

Cleaning service

There are some animals that give a cleaning service to others. A cleaner helps its host by removing fragments of food or parasites and in return gets a free meal for its trouble.

◁ A cattle egret pecks delicately near the eye of a cow. The egret is looking for ticks that feed on the blood of the cow.

△ Oxpeckers love to pick out and eat parasites found on large animals. These ones are looking for an easy meal in the creases of the thick hide of a black rhinoceros.

Delicate shrimp clean the gills of a beautiful copper band butterfly-fish. ▷

Invertebrates

Invertebrates clean themselves to keep their bodies in the best condition possible. Instead of having skin, feathers or scales, insects have a hard outer skeleton and use their legs or mouth parts to remove debris from their bodies.

◁ A raft spider cleans its front legs using its mouth parts.

Even small ants take time to groom themselves. This bulldog ant is cleaning its antennae before moving on to other parts of its body. ▷

A cuckoo-bee grips a plant stem with its strong jaws while it cleans itself with its legs. ▷

As it travels from flower to flower, the bee picks up grains of pollen on its hairy coat. It combs the pollen from its body and takes it to the nest in tiny baskets on its hind legs. This bee is removing pollen from its mouth parts. ▽

Glossary

Antennae The feelers of an insect.

Bond Something that brings animals together.

Cemented Joined together firmly.

Debris Loose, unwanted material.

Dominant Most important or most powerful.

Forepaws The two front paws.

Grooming Paying care and attention to the surface of the body by washing, licking, and scratching, for example.

Insects Small, six-legged creatures with wings and a body divided into sections.

Invertebrates Animals that have no backbone. Insects, spiders, clams, worms, and sponges are all invertebrates.

Mammal An animal whose females give birth to live young which they feed with milk from their bodies.

Mites Types of small parasites.

Mutual Shared.

Parasites Small animals that live on another animal without giving anything back in return.

Pollen The powder of flowers.

Roost A perch from which a bat rests or on which a bird sits.

Saliva The liquid that forms in the mouth.

Skeleton The body framework of an animal.

Supple Bending easily.

Books to read

Bennett, Paul. *Making a Nest.* New York: Thomson Learning, 1994.

Burton, Jane. *Keeping Clean.* Milwaukee, WI: Gareth Stevens, 1989.

Hornblow, Leonora & Arthur Hornblow. *Animals do the Strangest Things.* New York: Random House Books for Young Readers, 1990

Projects

Project one: **Garden wildlife (or local park)**

Keeping clean is an important part of an animal's life. There are many animals, both large and small, that you can observe keeping clean. If you have a bird bath, record how long each bird spends bathing and preening. A bird cannot fly properly if its feathers are not in good condition. They must even bathe in the winter too. Watch birds bathing in a rain-filled gutter or even a puddle. Record all your observations (including photographs) in your wildlife diary.

See if you can find any small creatures keeping clean. Spiders can be seen cleaning their mouth parts and legs. Butterflies, ants, and house flies also clean themselves. Have a good look around your backyard and see what animals you can observe. How do they keep themselves clean? Do they bathe, use their mouths, or use their legs to keep clean? Record all your observations and drawings in your wildlife diary.

Project two: **Pets**

If you or your friends have any pets you can watch them to see how they keep themselves clean. Dogs, cats, and birds spend a lot of time cleaning themselves and so do gerbils, mice, and rabbits. You may even have a more unusual pet such as a snake, lizard, or stick insect. How do they keep clean? Record all your observations, including drawings and photographs, in your wildlife diary.

Index